D0467944

My Poet

In memory of Mary Oliver
(1935–2019)

and for Emily
with love,
—P. M.

To the memory of my fifth-grade teacher,
Mr. Carino, poetry enthusiast, nature lover,
and exceptional human being
—J. H.

Katherine Tegen Books is an imprint of HarperCollins Publishers.

My Poet
Text copyright © 2022 by Patricia MacLachlan
Illustrations copyright © 2022 by Jen Hill
All rights reserved. Manufactured in Italy.
No part of this book may be used or reproduced in any manner whatsoever
without written permission except in the case of brief quotations embodied in
critical articles and reviews. For information address HarperCollins Children's Books,
 a division of HarperCollins Publishers, 195 Broadway, New York, NY 10007.
     www.harpercollinschildrens.com
     Library of Congress Control Number: 2021941524
       ISBN 978-0-06-297114-2
         The artist used gouache to create the illustrations for this book.
           Typography by Amy Ryan
             22 23 24 25 26 RTLO   10 9 8 7 6 5 4 3 2 1
                    ❖
                 First Edition

MacLachlan, Patricia,
My poet /
[2022]
333052549532
gi   10/24/22

My Poet

by PATRICIA MacLACHLAN

Pictures by JEN HILL

KT KATHERINE TEGEN BOOKS
An Imprint of HarperCollins Publishers

*I*t's the first day of summer vacation.
I walk to the farmers market,
with the poet who lives next door.
I call her "my poet."

She taps my pocket.

"What's there, Lucy?"

I hold up my small notebook and pen.

"I'm looking for words," I say.

"Me, too," says my poet.

At the market a little boy picks up a
   round red strawberry.
"Strawberry!" he says to my poet.
She picks up a strawberry too.
"Jewel!" she tells him.
The little boy grins.
Where does that word "jewel" come from?

Later we walk by the sea
with her dogs—
small woolly white,
the curly-coated black,
with his dog smile,
tongue out.

How does my poet hear the words
she writes about them?

Does she find words in their fur?

Does she hear their dog talk,
read their thoughts?

Does she see the word "joy" in them?

We gather sand in our hands. I pour
a handful into her hand, my poet
letting it slip through fingers,
smiling,
knowing something.
Does the sand whisper to her?

She puts her face in the wild rugosa roses.

Do the roses sing words?

I put my face there.

    I sneeze.

She picks up a round white stone,
smoothed by the sea,
closing my hand over it—
warm from *her* hand.
"It has a story, Lucy," my poet tells me.
What story is that?

Does the blue heron who flies over my poet
in a darkening sky
carry words to her
in his high cry?

I watch my poet in the woods
by the marsh.
Does she untangle the sound of
aspen leaves
blowing in the wind
into words?

Rain begins—

a clap of thunder.

Rain gentle at first,

then hard.

We hold hands and run

to a boathouse.

"Look," I say, pointing.

A spider spinning a web

of lace.

"Words?" I ask her.

"Of course," she says.

I stare at the spider in her web.

I surprise myself.

"Quiet and quick,

    spinning the words of my web," I say.

My poet smiles at me. She is not surprised.

She puts out her hand.

I lay my hand on hers.

Does the red fox living under my porch
come out to offer her words?
I follow the poet,
who watches the fox.

I listen.

I do not hear them speak.

Does the horse my poet writes about
running to the fence
whinny words to the poet
as he puts his face on hers,
loving her?

My poet writes of the fish in a warm pond,
swimming around her feet,
coming out to nibble tender grasses.
Do they bring her tender words?

In the summer dusk I sit on my porch
    with my notebook and pen.
I see my poet in her open window
    as she writes.

She waves at me.
And she comes over to sit on the top step.
"Are you writing something, Lucy?" she asks.
"I'm still looking for the words," I say.
She puts her hand on her head,
    then over her heart.

"The words are here," she says. "You just

    have to find them."

And I know the secret!

She listens.

She touches.

    But the words are hers.

    And the words can be mine.

She touches my white sea stone.

"Your stone," she says.

I shake my head.

"My *jewel*!" I say.

She laughs.

"You're finding your words," she says.

And when my poet goes home,
   I write.

Sea Stone
You came through the cold
warmed by my poet's hand,
and mine,
to be kept warm
forever.

Lucy

Author's Note

For years I have known the magic of the poet Mary Oliver: her love of the natural world—the landscape of Cape Cod and the sea, the ponds, the woods, and her affection for her dogs. Mary Oliver was a beloved writer who wrote many books of poetry and prose. She won numerous awards, including the National Book Award and the Pulitzer Prize.

Mary wrote fondly of her dog Percy, who "ate a book."

She appreciated children too. Once, in a Truro market, I saw a small boy hold up a strawberry to show her.

"Strawberry," he said.

Mary picked up a strawberry and whispered something to him, making him laugh and laugh.

"She's the poet," the owner said to me. I knew. Mary Oliver and I were not close friends, but we crossed paths—smiled at the post office, waving as we both walked our dogs.

And I live in her magic, reading her poems over and over.

Her landscape is my landscape, too.

—P.M.